ABC's Of Anarchy

By

Brian Heagney

This book is cared for by:

_____

ISBN: 1453687815
EAN-13: 9781453687819

All images and graphics drawn by Brian Charles Heagney

The font used throughout most of this book is "1550", available for free from www.fontstock.com, except in the cases of the "U" and "J" which use a font called "3000", which is also available for free from www.fontstock.com
(otherwise, the "U" and "J" would look like "V" and "I", respectively).

Additionally, the font Times New Roman is used for the large letters appearing on the top left portion of all of the graphics within this book.

This book was created using:
The OpenOffice Suite (available at www.openoffice.org)
The Gimp image editor (available at www.gimp.org)
Inkscape (available at www.inkscape.org)
and Scribus Desktop Publishing software (available at www.scribus.net)
all open source and available for free.

Any likeness or resemblance to anyone alive or dead is purely intentional, you know who you are.

www.brianheagney.com

10 9 8 7 6 5 4 3 2 1

Acknowledgements:

Many people helped me with deciding on words, imagery, and text for this book. Whether you knew that this was a work in progress and offered constructive criticism, or you sent me hatemail and told me I should go back in time and stop myself from creating this, I appreciate all your suggestions.

So, a big thanks to the following:

Adam Feuer, Adelaide Anarchist Communist Group, Alex McFarland, Alissa Fogg, Barry Wilson, Becky Ray, Bill Davis, Bill Maley, Boff Whaley (for your thoughtful response and words of encouragement so early in this project), Brian Maloney, Chris Roose, Christine Fisher, Corvid Irata, Courtney Forrester, Cristy Road, Denise Kiernan, Donald Strickland (who is not only an incredible Step-Father, but was the best high school English teacher I could have asked for), Emily Clancy, enkiam, Jack Shuler, Dave Heagney, David Grimsley, Eric Haines, Geoff Guyette, Gina Castanzo Ferraro, Heather Heagney, Hilary Coon, Jack Shuler, Jae Holloway, James Quinn, Jason Deeming, Jessica Furst, Joan Heagney, Jodi Staley, Joe Capristo, John L., Jonathan Henderson, Kas Sandra, Kathleen Heagney Pittelkau (for all of your support throughout the years), Katie Yow, Keith Farnish, Kristen Droesch, Kymber Owens, Leigh Meyers, Lior Yaani, Lissa Carter, Liz Seymour, Lu Randall, Mark Dixon, Mark Hosler (especially for those last-minute words of advice), Mary Malpass Sorel, Mary Smart, Matt Harris, Mauriah Conway-Spatola, Mira Dolinar, Maura Hurley, Nicca Tapping, Niels Strandskov, Nikki Craft, Nora Bradbury-Haehl, Paul Hart, Phillip Vanbell, Rachel Shaw, Rahula Janowski, Ramsey Kanann, Ran Prieur, Raphi Rechitsky, my amazing wife Renee Heagney, Rob los Ricos, Roland Jesperson, Roxanne Amico, Roxanne Baker, Sandra Dodd, Sarah Coffey, Sarah Morris, Scott DeMuth, Sess, Sharp Hall, Sydney Steiger, Sue Coe (especially for the last-minute editing advice), supersheep, my awesome mother Susan Strickland, Talia Felony, Terry Hammond, trsight, TruthElixir, Virginia Freeman Dupont, and Yuthika Kim.

And I am very thankful for moral support from most of those mentioned above and additionally:

Anna Lena, Asa Anna Newell, Beth Joyce, Crystal Bright, Daniel Summers, Gwyneth Cliver, Hannah Hawkins, Heather Tedder, Ian Joyce, Jen Heagney, Jo Boykin, Joseph Camann, Julia Haverstock, Liz Seymour, Lori Heffner Gibson, Mollie Howey, Nancy VanBell, Natalie Turner, Pete Turner, Stephanie Melesky, Suebear Hebner, Todd Fisher, Willie Repoley, and all of those anarchists from Greensboro, North Carolina whom I have failed to mention here.

I want to tell you about anarchism.

I want to tell you about anarchism because I think that it is well that you should know all about it.

I want to tell you about anarchism because everything that you have heard about it is wrong.

I want to tell you about anarchism because I believe anarchism is the finest and neatest thing that has ever been invented.

I want to tell you about anarchism because anarchism is the only thing that can give you liberty and well-being and bring peace and joy to the world.

-The Weatherman
(paraphrasing Alexander Berkman)
From The ABC's of Anarchism
a collaborative work by Negativland and Chumbawamba

A note to the reader:

So, what the heck is **anarchy**, anyway?

The word **anarchy** comes from the Greek **an** (meaning **without**) and **arkhos** (meaning ... or **ruler**). And the Greek prefix **Arkhi-**, while not the documented root of the **anarchy**, means **master** or **chief**. In any case, **anarchy** literally means **without leaders**, or **without rulers**, or **without masters**.

Applying the concept of **no masters** to your life can take shape in an infinite number of ways, and not everyone will agree on how to go about it. Can you be an anarchist and submit to the will of God? Can you be an anarchist and own property? Can you be an anarchist and pay taxes to a nation-state? Can you be an anarchist and be a proponent of civilization and technological advancements? Can you be an anarchist and raise well adjusted children?

I'm not going to answer those questions, both for the sake of brevity, and so I don't rile even more anarchists than I already have. But some anarchists have taken sides and formed various versions of anarchy based on answers to the questions above, thereby creating anarch-ISMS. These anarchisms have commonly held beliefs and doctrines, and it follows that some anarchisms may be the complete opposite of other anarchisms.

Luckily, this isn't a book about anarchism - I don't know or care enough about all the different branches of anarchism just yet. This is a book about anarchy, living a life without masters. So, the following pages are full of examples of applying anarchy to your life in various ways. Undoubtedly, not all anarchists will condone or even like this book. And not everyone will even like the way I've just defined **anarchy**. That's okay. Hopefully, there will soon be many **ABC's of Anarchy** books on the market, so we can once and for all rid the world of the negative connotations of that beautiful word, **Anarchy**.

Lastly, even though I sought out input from many people (anarchist and non-anarchist, experts and novices, friends and foes), and even though I've been working on this book for the past two years, I am still seeing things I want to change. I would love to turn C into "Class War", G into "Gentrification, and U into "Utopia", for example. I also want to change the Y page to a word that better exemplefies anarchy, and perhaps rewrite all of the text, or have a real writer take a stab at it. (I should also probably rewrite this little introduction too.) I hope you can forgive such glaring ommissions, and please contact me with all of your questions, comments and concerns.

- Brian Heagney
www.brianheagney.com

for
Maeve Adele

A is for Anarchy

The word Anarchy literally means "without rulers", "without leaders", or "without masters". Any definition more or less than that is a matter of personal opinion. You might apply anarchy to your life in a way that is completely different from anyone else.

What masters do you have in your life?

What would a world without masters be like?

B b is for Black Bloc

A black bloc is a group of people dressed in black to represent either mass solidarity for a cause, or mass resistance to oppression.

For what cause would you gather your friends together in a black bloc?

How can joining together in a black bloc help anything?

C is for Critical Mass

Critical Mass is an informal direct action involving a leaderless group travelling through town on bicycles or other human powered vehicles. Some participants may want to show support for safe bicycle travel on the roads, others may just want to get together for a nice bike ride with friends.

What kinds of vehicles do you use regularly?

Where is the farthest place you have walked or cycled to?

D is for D.I.Y.

D.I.Y. stands for Do It Yourself. You don't always have to rely on experts or professionals; you are an amazing person with many talents and skills, with the brains to learn how to do anything you want.

What sorts of projects can you do by yourself?

What is something you want to learn to do by yourself?

E e is for Egalitarian

In an egalitarian system, all people have equal access or opportunity to power and resources.

Whom do you feel more or less important than?

Why might someone want to have more power than someone else?

F f is for Food Not Bombs

Food Not Bombs is a gathering of people who believe that no one should ever go hungry. Every week local Food Not Bombs chapters obtain free food to cook and share with anyone who wants it.

Would you ever consider eating food that has been thrown into the garbage?

What is the longest amount of time that you have gone hungry?

G g is for Gender Role

The term Gender Role refers to how society expects you to behave based on your sex. In reality, however, few behaviors or preferences are determined by whether you are a boy or a girl.

Why do you think some toys and activities are considered either masculine or feminine?

What are some toys or activities that you don't associate with any gender?

H is for Hierarchy

Hierarchy is a systematic tool for organizing people or things for the purposes of assigning order and importance, achieving a goal, or deconstructing and understanding a concept or issue.

How do you
organize your daily activities?

How do you and your family make decisions?

I i

is for Infoshop

An infoshop is a place where you can go to find radical books and zines, learn about local events, attend workshops and readings, and sometimes even catch punk-rock shows.

What was the last book you read? What was it about?

Where do you go to find out what is happening in your community?

J j is for Job

A job is work one does in exchange for money. Many people work a job eight or more hours of the day, drastically reducing the number of hours they have to enjoy life with their family and friends.

What is the difference between work you do for fun, and work you do because someone tells you to?

What do you think would happen if everyone suddenly quit their jobs?

K is for Kabouter

Kabouter is the Dutch word for "gnome", and also the name taken by a group of Dutch anarchists who used pranks, civil disobedience, and sabotage to expose problems like police brutality, housing shortages, and the destruction of the environment. The Kabouters became so popular that people even voted them to serve in the local City Council.

Vote Kabouter

Opération Wandering Branch

If you thought something was wrong with your community, how could you tell people about it?

What is an example of a prank that could help inform, educate or amuse people?

L is for Liberation Front

Liberation is the state of complete freedom. A Liberation Front is a group of people determined to help others attain a life of freedom. Liberation Fronts have been formed to aid animals, oppressed people, the Earth, and even billboards.

Why might anything or anyone need help being liberated?

How can you support others who are attempting to liberate themselves?

M
m

is for Mutual Aid

Mutual Aid is the voluntary sharing
of resources and services.

Describe a time when you helped someone in need.

What are some resources or services you can offer
other people?

N n is for Nihilism

Nihilism is the rejection of traditional values. A Nihilist may choose to build his or her own cultural system of morals from scratch in order to reflect the needs and desires of current society.

Describe some traditions or other aspects of your culture that may not make sense in your life.

What are some traditions or morals that you would choose to include in your cultural world?

O is for Organize

To organize means to create order or systematize things to accomplish goals and objectives. Organizing may involve assigning tasks, establishing directives, or creating charts, maps and documents.

What sorts of activities do you enjoy that are organized?

Describe a situation which would be better if things weren't organized.

P p is for Propaganda

Propaganda is any type of media that is created specifically to further the doctrines or principles of an organization or movement. At best propoganda is informative and thought-provoking; at worst it is deceptive and damaging.

In what way is this book a piece of propaganda?

What sorts of propaganda do you encounter during an average day?

Q is for Question Authority

Authority refers to anyone or thing in the position of imposing power over you. To question authority means to ask questions or express views or opinions that differ from those of an authority figure.

To whom have you decided to look for advice, leadership and guidance?

Describe a time you corrected or questioned someone who had more expereince than you.

R r is for Rewild

Rewilding means learning to live without any tools or artifacts of civilization. Some rewilding activities include foraging, hunting, fire-making, and building primitive structures.

Describe something you know how to make from scratch.

Why might someone believe that modern civilization has been harmful to ourselves and our world?

S is for Squat

A squat is an empty, vacant, or neglected structure that someone has decided to turn into a living space.

What makes a house or apartment a home?

How do you think the very first people bought property, and from whom did they buy it?

T is for Train-Hopping

Train-Hopping is the art of sneaking onto trains and riding to your destination for free. While train-hopping, you can see some amazing parts of the country that you might not normally experience.

To where might you like to hop a train?

What sorts of difficulties do you think you would encounter while train-hopping across the country?

U is for Un-School

U u

Un-schooling is the process of children learning from real-world, hands-on, self-guided experiences, rather than from a classroom setting. Parents involved in un-schooling recognize that all children love to learn, and do so best when following their own instincts.

What are some things you would do if you chose to stop attending school?

What is one activity you have planned for yourself to do this week?

V is for Voluntary Participation

Voluntary Participation is actively choosing to be a part of something. As a liberated being, you have the right and obligation to act of your own free will, to participate in activities on a consentual basis.

Describe a situation where someone might try to force you to do something you don't want to do.

What are some consequences of asserting your right to voluntarily participate?

W is for Without Borders

A border is something that divides one area from another. Dictators and Nation-States divide the world into political zones as they see fit. However, viewing the Earth from space, we see a world without political borders, a world where the only boundaries are the great mountains and the vast seas.

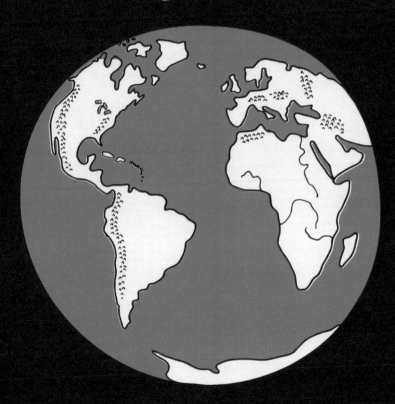

What are some naturally ocurring borders you encounter on a daily basis?

What are some human-made borders you encounter on a daily basis?

X is for Xylography

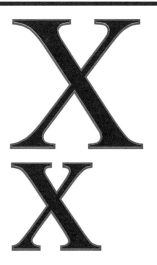

Xylography is the art of printmaking by woodcutting. Lots of propaganda (especially anarchist propaganda) has been produced using Xylography.

What was the last picture you drew?

What are all of the different ways you have made pieces of art?

Y is for Youth Hostel

A Youth Hostel is an inexpensive alternative to a hotel. When spending the night at a Youth Hostel, you might stay in a large room with many people. Fortunately, this enables you to meet new friends and share interesting stories.

What might be some differences between spending the night on your own versus sharing a room with many other people?

When are some times you would rather sleep alone, and when might you prefer to sleep in a room with others?

Z is for Zine

A zine is a kind of mini-magazine. Zines can be completely hand-made, or they can be photocopied.

Z Z

A zine might be: a DIY manual; a collection of poetry or short stories; a personalized historical account; a collection of recipes; a boring political tract; or anything else you can think of!

Which of the zines above would you like to read today?

If you were going to make a zine, what would it be about?

is for _____

Do you think there could be a new letter for our alphabet? Now is your opportunity to make one up. And if you want to, draw a picture for it!

Can you come up with a sound that doesn't have a letter in our alphabet?

How do you think the alphabet was invented?

Made in the USA
Charleston, SC
13 July 2011